YORK
TRAVEL GUIDE 2025

DISCOVER THE BEAUTY OF YORKSHIRE, ENGLAND, A REGION STEEPED IN HISTORY AND NATURAL WONDER

NEW EDITION

TRAVEL GUIDE

Louis R. Anderson

All Right Reserved

No part of this book may be produced, stored in a retrieval system. or transmitted in any form or by any means, electronic or mechanical, photocopying, recording or otherwise, without the prior writing permission of the copyright owner.

Copyright © Louis R. Anderson

Disclaimer

The world is constantly changing, hotels change ownership or close, restaurants might adjust their prices, museum could alter their closing hours, and transportation routes can be modified.

This changes can happen even after our author have visited. inspected and written about these places

While we strive to keep all information as current as possible: some changes may inevitable occur before a new edition of this guidebook is published.

Thanks you for choosing our guidebook, we hope you have an amazing trip.

ABOUT THE AUTHOR

Raised on a steady diet of history books, hiking boots, and train station daydreams, the author of this guide has spent years weaving through the cobbled streets and countryside trails of Europe—always with a notebook in one hand and a camera in the other. York, however, holds a special place in their heart. It's a city they first visited on a rainy spring morning and never quite forgot. The layers of Roman stone, Viking lore, and medieval magic cast a spell that turned a casual visit into a lifelong fascination.

With a professional background in travel writing and a deep love for storytelling, the author brings together personal insight, local tips, and a traveler's eye for detail. They don't believe in shallow sightseeing or copy-paste recommendations. Every entry in this guide is rooted in firsthand experience, tested itineraries, and conversations with the people who make York more than just a postcard-perfect destination.

Whether traveling solo, planning a family adventure, or returning to York for the second or third time, readers will find in this guide not just facts—but the feeling of walking alongside a fellow explorer who wants you to truly feel the city, not just check it off a list.

Their mission? To help every traveler—first-timer or seasoned globe-trotter—fall in love with York on their own terms and leave with not just photos, but stories worth remembering.

GRATITUDE

Creating this guide to York has been a journey shaped not just by stone-paved streets and soaring cathedrals, but by people—kind, passionate, curious people who made the city come alive in unexpected ways.

First, thank you to the locals of York who never hesitated to offer a story, a smile, or directions when I looked a bit too lost down one of the city's winding alleys. The way you protect your heritage while welcoming strangers is a quiet magic that deserves every bit of admiration.

To the travelers I met—on walking tours, in cafés, at bus stops—you reminded me that no two York journeys are ever the same. Your questions, laughter, and even frustrations helped shape this book into something more thoughtful and practical.

I'm deeply grateful to the small business owners, museum guides, pub staff, and guesthouse hosts who patiently answered my endless questions, shared historical facts with genuine pride, and always managed to slip in a bit of local humor.

To the readers who trust this guide to shape their adventure—thank you. Your time, curiosity, and willingness to explore mean everything. If even one moment of your trip feels smoother, deeper, or more memorable because of this book, then every late-night rewrite and chilly early-morning note-taking session was worth it.

And lastly, thank you to the city of York itself—for being timeless and surprising in equal measure. This book is for you, and because of you.

TABLE OF CONTENT

Chapter 1 10

Start Here: Why York Captivates Every Type of Traveler 10

    A Powerful Welcome from the Author: What to Expect and How to Use This Book 13

    What Makes York Uniquely Different in 2025 15

    How This Guide Prevents Travel Mistakes and Missed Opportunities 16

Chapter 2 19

York at a Glance: The City's Heart in 24 Minutes 19

    A Visual and Verbal Orientation: The Shape of the City 20

    Best Time to Visit York (Tailored by Travel Purpose) 24

Chapter 3 27

Arrival Smart: How to Get to York Easily & Stress-Free 27

    Best Transport Routes to York from Major Cities & Airports 28

    Arriving in York: Station Tips, Taxis, and Walking Routes 31

    York Pass, Train Deals & Local Bus Hacks (2025 Updates) 32

    Mistakes to Avoid When Arriving 33

Chapter 4 35

Where to Stay in York: Area Guide for All Budgets & Styles 35

    Interactive Lodging Map: Match Your Style to the Right York Neighborhood 36

    Best Accommodation Types for Every Style & Budget 40

    Airbnb vs Hotel vs B&B: Pros, Cons & Hidden Costs 42

    Safety, Noise Zones & Walkability Tips 43

Chapter 5 45

York's Essentials in 1–5 Days: Complete Daily Itineraries with Custom Maps 45

One Day in York: The Blitz Tour (Perfect for First-Timers & Day-Trippers) 46

Three Days in York: The Explorer's Route 48

Five Days in York: The Deep Dive 50

Don't-Miss Tips: Best Times for Photos & Fewer Crowds 52

Chapter 6 54

Immersive York: Top Attractions, Hidden Gems & Living History 54

Major attractions (York Minster, Jorvik Viking Centre, The Shambles) explained without fluff 55

Book tickets online in advance—queues are long year-round. 57

Lesser-Known Museums & Off-Grid History 59

Ethical Travel: Supporting York with Respect 60

Chapter 7 62

Eat Like a Local: Pubs, Afternoon Teas, Bakeries & Beyond 62

Iconic Foods to Try in York 63

Best Places for Traditional Yorkshire Cuisine 65

Vegan, Halal, Kosher, Gluten-Free & Budget Dining 66

Dining Etiquette, Tipping Norms & Menu Terms 68

Chapter 8 71

Shop, Stroll, Snap: Markets, Boutiques & Instagram Spots 71

The best local markets (Shambles Market, Bishopthorpe Road indie scene) 72

Vintage, Rare Books & Artisan Shopping 74

How to Shop Smart and Pack it Back Home 77

Chapter 9 79

York Beyond the Centre: Day Trips, Countryside & Coastal Escapes ... 79

The Classics: Unmissable Day Trips from York 80

How to Travel Without the Stress 83

Cultural Etiquette Outside the City 84

Itinerary A: 1-Day North Moors Loop (by Car) 85

Chapter 10 87

Stay Confident: Practical Tips, Local Etiquette & Travel Smart 87

Staying Connected: Internet Access, SIM Cards & Power Plugs 88

Travel Safety, Medical Help & Insurance in the UK 89

Local Etiquette: How to Respect York's Historical and Religious Spaces 90

LGBTQ+ Travel Tips: Welcoming, Safe, and Celebratory 91

Avoiding Tourist Traps & Common Scams in 2025 93

Chapter 11 96

Conclusion: Your York Adventure Starts Now 96

Final Travel Wisdom for First-Timers 97

Encouragement to Slow Down & Savor York's Stories 98

How to Leave York With No Regrets 99

Resources for Further Reading, Travel Tools & Local Tours 100

Chapter 12 103

Frequently Asked Questions (FAQs) – York Travel Guide 2025 103

GENERAL TRAVEL QUESTIONS 104

7 | York Travel Guide 2025

ARRIVAL & TRANSPORTATION 105

ACCOMMODATION & AREAS TO STAY 106

FOOD, DRINK & DINING ETIQUETTE 106

MONEY, INTERNET & PRACTICAL TIPS 107

SAFETY, HEALTH, INSURANCE & EMERGENCIES 108

INCLUSION, LGBTQ+ & ACCESSIBILITY 109

WELCOME TO YORK

Chapter 1

Start Here: Why York Captivates Every Type of Traveler

I still remember the first time I arrived in York. It wasn't my first trip to England, nor my first medieval city—but something about York instantly felt different. I'd just stepped off the train at York Station, expecting another charming British town. But what greeted me was a living storybook. A city where time folds into itself. Where you don't just walk the streets—you feel their weight, their rhythm, their echo.

York doesn't compete for attention. It doesn't beg to impress. It simply is. A city of presence.

For the seasoned traveler, York is a rare reward. It's not flashy or artificial. It's quietly rich—dripping with authenticity in every crooked timber, every cobbled path, every church bell echoing through narrow lanes. For the first-time visitor to England, it's the perfect capsule: a taste of Roman roads, Viking raids, and Victorian elegance, all within walking distance. It's a place that doesn't require you to "find the magic." It hands it to you.

You see, York is not a city that offers its wonders in neon or noise. Its treasures reveal themselves slowly—when you least expect them. A forgotten archway between bookshops. A centuries-old chocolate recipe passed down like folklore. A ghost story told by a guide who genuinely believes it. Or a saxophonist playing under the shadow of York Minster, his notes floating into the twilight.

You don't just "see" York. You inhabit it.

And that's what makes this place so powerfully personal. Everyone discovers their own version of York. For the romantic, it's moonlight walks along the city walls and candlelit dinners in ancient inns. For the history lover, it's the bones of Roman barracks beneath your feet, and Viking helmets waiting behind glass. For the spiritual traveler, it's the cathedral that humbles you into silence. For foodies, it's gravy-rich roast dinners in centuries-old pubs—and a sweet trail of sticky toffee and hand-whipped clotted cream.

Even for the solo wanderer, York is warm. It doesn't alienate you like a giant metropolis might. It invites you in. People talk here. They ask where you're from. They tell you where to go, but not like a tourist—they say it like a neighbor who wants you to feel at home.

I've traveled across Europe, wandered cities that proudly boast of their beauty, and yes—many live up to the hype. But York doesn't need to boast. It's already lived through empires, invasions, coronations, plagues, revolutions, and reinventions. And yet it remains utterly itself. It greets you like an old soul with stories to tell—if you're patient enough to listen.

This guide was created for travelers like you. Whether you're here to explore, escape, reconnect, or simply experience something real—I promise you, York will give you that. You'll leave with memories stitched into your senses. With photos, yes—but more importantly, with feelings.

So step in. Breathe it in. You're not just visiting York.

You're becoming a part of it.

A Powerful Welcome from the Author: What to Expect and How to Use This Book

Welcome to York Travel Guide 2025 — your honest, in-depth, and experience-driven companion to one of the most timeless cities in the world.

I'm thrilled you're holding this guide in your hands (or on your device screen). Whether you're planning your very first visit to York or returning after years away, I wrote this guide with you in mind — not as a distant observer behind a desk, but as someone who has walked the Shambles before sunrise, shared laughter with locals over a Yorkshire ale, and stood beneath York Minster with goosebumps on my arms and no words to say.

This isn't just a book. It's an invitation.

York isn't the kind of place you skim through. It's a city that deserves—and rewards—slow travel. You don't need to rush through it like a checklist of sights. You need to soak in its rhythm. Every corner tells a story, every alley holds a whisper of something you'd never know if you hurried past it. And this guide is designed to help you listen.

I want you to see more than what every tourist sees. I want you to discover the feeling of York. The silence of the cathedral's nave. The hush in a bookshop no bigger than a pantry. The laughter echoing from a pub garden. The strange comfort of a ghost tour in the rain. The pride in a local's eyes when they tell you about their city.

Here's how to use this book so you get every ounce of value it offers:

How to Navigate This Guide

This guide isn't meant to be read cover-to-cover in one sitting—though you're more than welcome to if you enjoy immersive travel reading. It's structured to give you freedom: freedom to flip to what you need now, and to return later for the details you didn't know you needed yet.

Each chapter is tailored to a specific stage or interest of your trip:

Planning Your Arrival? — Jump to the transportation and accommodation chapters.

Want to Know What Not to Miss? — The daily itineraries and attractions sections will save you time and stress.

Hungry and Curious? — You'll find authentic food spots, cultural etiquette, and recommendations from real locals.

Traveling on a Tight Budget? — Budget hacks, free sights, and walking routes are included to stretch your pounds without sacrificing experience.

Here for the First Time? — You'll get hand-holding without being talked down to.

A Repeat Visitor? — Discover the local secrets, day trips, and hidden histories most tourists never hear about.

Every section is written with empathy. I've anticipated your questions, your hesitations, even your fears.

I know what it's like to worry about wasting time, spending too much, getting lost, missing "the good stuff," or feeling like you're just following a crowd. This guide is built to remove those fears—and replace them with clarity, confidence, and joy.

There are no empty descriptions, no padded-out lists just to hit a word count, no recycled fluff from the internet. Every detail was selected, tested, and written with the traveler's real experience in mind.

What Makes York Uniquely Different in 2025

The year 2025 finds York in a special moment. It is no longer just "a charming old city" or "a historical stop" on a broader UK itinerary. York has transformed — not by changing its soul, but by deepening it. By leaning fully into its history, its stories, and its future.

You'll find a city that has preserved its ancient bones but wears a fresh face. You can walk the same walls Roman legions once patrolled, yet stop at a café run by a young barista who serves Yorkshire coffee sourced ethically from Kenya. You can buy handcrafted Viking jewelry made with 1,000-year-old techniques—just after scanning a QR code to access a virtual museum trail.

<u>In 2025, York is more than quaint. It's quietly cutting-edge.</u>

Sustainability is now built into tourism here. You'll find eco-certified accommodations, zero-waste markets, carbon-neutral walking tours, and river cruises powered by clean energy. York hasn't gone "green" to trend-chase—it's done it to preserve the city for the next 1,000 years.

York is also becoming a center for inclusive travel. Accessibility has improved significantly, with more ramps, more guided support for neurodiverse visitors, and gender-neutral facilities in public attractions. There are signs of real effort in every part of the city—not performative inclusivity, but thoughtful change.

Local pride is high. Unlike over-touristed destinations that are fraying at the edges, York's locals still want you to visit. They'll talk to you. They'll help you find your way. You'll see school children taking walking history lessons on the streets. You'll hear regional accents that haven't been softened for outsiders. You'll feel like you're entering a living, breathing community—not just a theme park wearing old clothes.

This balance of history and progress is what sets York apart in 2025. It's not just a place to take photos. It's a place to feel something. A place to slow down, lean in, and let a thousand years of stories wash over you.

How This Guide Prevents Travel Mistakes and Missed Opportunities

Let me be brutally honest with you: York is easy to underestimate. And that's how most travelers get it wrong.

They think they can "do York" in a few hours. They book a single night. They rush through a handful of attractions. They take pictures of the cathedral but never step inside. They see the Shambles but don't wander its side streets.

They miss the walks along the River Ouse at sunset. They don't know about the hidden art in Holy Trinity Church. They skip the tiny local bakeries in favor of chains. They follow the crowds and wonder why the magic feels out of reach.

This guide is here to stop that from happening to you.

Every section was crafted with the traveler's experience in mind. I've laid out daily itineraries that don't just tell you what to do—they tell you why to do it, when to do it, and how to do it without stress. You'll know which museums are best at what time of day, where to find clean toilets, how to avoid long queues, and what's genuinely worth your time and money.

There are no overwhelming lists of "Top 100 Things to Do" here. That's not helpful. Instead, you'll find curated routes, quiet spots to rest, locals-only secrets, and real-life tips that guidebooks and online blogs often miss.

I've also included frequent "Author's Notes" — personal insights from my own walks through York. Think of me as your invisible companion. When I say, "Take the side alley to the right of the church—it looks unremarkable but leads to the best chocolate shop in the city," that's not a tip you'll find on TripAdvisor. That's the voice of experience, trying to save you from an ordinary trip.

More importantly, this book is designed to work with how you travel. Whether you're a planner, a wanderer, or somewhere in between, you'll find flexibility. Use it in real time on the street or the night before over a pint.

Because you deserve more than just a **"nice trip."**

You deserve a York that becomes a core memory.

And that's exactly what this book aims to give you.

So, take a breath. Let's walk through York together. You're not just going to see it. You're going to feel it — and remember it for the rest of your life.

Chapter

2

York at a Glance: The City's Heart in 24 Minutes

You step out of York Station, and almost immediately you see it—that breathtaking Gothic spire rising into the sky. That's York Minster, calling you in like a lighthouse calls in ships. Around it, everything else gently unfolds: a compact city wrapped in medieval walls, stitched together by cobbled lanes and laced with riverside walks. You don't need a car here. You barely even need a map. York isn't just walkable—it's immersive. You're never more than a few steps away from something historic, something local, or something surprisingly delightful.

This chapter is your 24-minute crash course—a verbal orientation, if you like—to help you understand how York is laid out, what each area feels like, and what kind of experiences await you in each district. You won't need to second-guess your directions or wonder what's beyond the next street. This is where we get you rooted and ready.

A Visual and Verbal Orientation: The Shape of the City

Imagine York as a circle within a circle.

The inner circle is the historic City Centre, encased by ancient stone walls and medieval gates (called "bars"). That's where the action is: the Minster, The Shambles, the York Castle Museum, the Roman ruins, the best-known pubs, and most boutique shops and tearooms. Everything is tightly packed in, but not cramped. You can walk from one side of the City Centre to the other in under 20 minutes—though I dare you to try without stopping a dozen times along the way.

The outer circle—just beyond the walls—is where the city breathes. It's quieter, greener, more residential, but still deeply historical. This is where the locals live, where the best hidden cafés reside, and where you'll find character zones like Bootham, Clifton, Bishopthorpe Road, Micklegate, and Heworth.

Each of these areas has its own personality, like members of a family. Let's get to know them.

Quick Overview of York's Districts & Character Zones

City Centre (Inside the Walls)

This is the beating heart of York. It's where most visitors spend the majority of their time—and for good reason. You'll find:

York Minster – The city's spiritual and architectural crown jewel

The Shambles – A narrow, crooked medieval street, rumored to inspire Diagon Alley in Harry Potter

Clifford's Tower – A Norman-era tower offering panoramic city views

Museum Gardens – A tranquil green space with ruins, squirrels, and picnic-perfect lawns

Stonegate & Petergate – Shopping streets packed with charm, history, and hidden pubs

Vibe: Lively, atmospheric, always buzzing.

Best For: First-timers, romantic walks, shopping, architecture, culture.

Bootham

Just north of the city walls, Bootham feels like the elegant older cousin of York. It stretches from Bootham Bar to the leafy edges of Clifton, lined with Georgian townhouses and art galleries.

Highlights: Close to York Minster, Bootham School, and the York Art Gallery

Hidden Gem: No. 88 Walmgate – A local favorite café tucked into a former apothecary

Top Stay: The Grange Hotel – A grand townhouse hotel with historic interiors

Vibe: Refined, quiet, upscale.

Best For: Couples, art lovers, peaceful stays, walking access to the centre.

Clifton

Go a little further out and you hit Clifton—a green, spacious district that feels suburban but remains deeply connected to York's soul. It borders the River Ouse, making it a wonderful place for riverside strolls or picnics.

Highlights: Clifton Bridge, Homestead Park, and the York Observatory

Local Secret: Clifton Ings – A floodplain and nature reserve with great sunset views

Top Tip: Bring binoculars; it's a birdwatcher's paradise.

Vibe: Relaxed, natural, community-focused.

Best For: Nature lovers, families, peaceful picnics, long river walks.

Bishopthorpe Road ("Bishy Road")

Ask any local where they hang out on weekends, and chances are they'll say Bishy Road. This area is south of the city, popular for its independent shops, cafes, and creative energy.

Highlights: Rowntree Park, The Pig & Pastry café, monthly local markets

Local Favorite: Robinsons – A cozy brunch spot with a cult following

Seasonal Joy: Cherry blossoms and daffodils bloom thick in springtime

Vibe: Trendy, local, bohemian.

Best For: Foodies, solo travelers, slow mornings, creative inspiration.

Micklegate

Cross the bridge from the train station and you're on Micklegate—the historic royal entrance to York. Monarchs once entered the city through Micklegate Bar. Today, it's known for its pubs, boutique hotels, and lively nightlife.

Highlights: Bar Convent Living Heritage Centre, several award-winning pubs

Historic Note: Heads of traitors were once displayed on the gatehouse

Try This: The Falcon Tap beer garden—hidden, but worth the hunt

Vibe: Historic but fun, slightly gritty in the best way.

Best For: Pub crawlers, history buffs, young couples, repeat visitors.

Heworth

East of the city lies Heworth—a quiet, residential area with wide streets, Victorian homes, and a slower pace of life. If you're staying longer or want a break from crowds, this is your spot.

Highlights: Monk Stray (expansive common land), quiet cafés, good B&Bs

Bonus: Easy access to the Minster without the traffic

Stay Here If: You want peace, morning runs, or a long-term stay

Vibe: Local, unpretentious, residential.

Best For: Families, digital nomads, long-term stays, older travelers.

Best Time to Visit York (Tailored by Travel Purpose)

There's no wrong time to visit York—but there is a right time for you. Here's how to decide when to go based on your travel goals:

For Photographers & Instagrammers: Late April to early May

The cherry blossoms are blooming, bluebells pop in Museum Gardens, and golden hour lasts longer.

Early mornings offer misty river shots and empty streets.

For Budget Travelers: Mid-January to early March

Lowest accommodation prices.

Fewer crowds in museums, and off-season deals at restaurants.

Downside: colder weather, shorter daylight—but still charming.

For Festival-Goers: February (JORVIK Viking Festival), July (York Early Music Festival), December (Christmas Markets)

Book accommodations early.

The city buzzes with energy, costumed events, street performances, and guided heritage tours.

For Romance Seekers: September and December

Autumn foliage in the parks, warm pubs with fireplaces, and candlelit restaurants.

December adds fairy lights, carol singers, and mulled wine magic.

For Solo Travelers & Story Seekers: October or March

Moderate crowds, introspective mood, cheaper rates.

Great for wandering without noise.

Excellent for ghost walks and self-reflection strolls on the city walls.

For History Lovers: Year-round

York's history doesn't depend on the weather.

But indoor attractions like the York Castle Museum and DIG are perfect for rainy days (which do happen).

Choose shoulder months (March, October, November) for better access and lower prices.

Your 24-Minute Summary

York is not a city to be "done." It's to be lived, felt, and wandered. Whether you base yourself in the vibrant City Centre or the leafy charm of Bishopthorpe Road, you'll always be within touching distance of the city's thousand-year story.

Think of this chapter as your compass. You now know where to go, what each part of York offers, and when to experience it at its best.

The rest of this guide will show you how to walk it, taste it, feel it, and take it with you—long after you've gone.

York isn't just a place on your map. It's about to become a piece of your memory. Let's dive deeper.

Chapter 3

Arrival Smart: How to Get to York Easily & Stress-Free

The first time I traveled to York from London, I was full of excitement—but also a bit frazzled. I had booked the cheapest train I could find, didn't realize the difference between King's Cross and St. Pancras, and lugged my suitcase past the same café twice trying to find the platform. When I finally arrived in York, I exited the wrong side of the station and spent 20 minutes dragging my bag around cobbled streets in the rain before realizing the Minster was in the opposite direction.

Learn from me: York doesn't require stress. In fact, it actively resists it—if you arrive smart.

This chapter will walk you through exactly how to get to York without the confusion, delay, or overwhelm. Whether you're coming from within the UK or flying in internationally, this section covers everything you need to know to start your York adventure smoothly.

Best Transport Routes to York from Major Cities & Airports

York is extremely well-connected. Situated almost perfectly between London and Edinburgh, it's part of the East Coast Main Line, one of the UK's fastest and most scenic rail routes. Whether you're arriving from a major city or stepping off a plane, you'll find multiple transport options.

From International Airports

From London Heathrow (LHR)

Step 1: Take the Heathrow Express to London Paddington (15 min).

Step 2: Tube from Paddington to King's Cross Station (30–40 min).

Step 3: Train from King's Cross to York (1h 50m on direct service).

Total Journey Time: ~3 to 3.5 hours.

From Manchester Airport (MAN)

Direct train to York: Departs every hour, no transfers needed.

Time: Around 1h 45m to 2 hours.

Tip: Book in advance for best prices; last-minute airport fares are costly.

From Leeds Bradford Airport (LBA)

Step 1: Take the Flyer A1 bus to Leeds City Centre (~30 minutes).

Step 2: Train from Leeds to York (~25 minutes).

Tip: Leeds is closer to York than Manchester or London, so this is a great option if you can fly into LBA.

From Edinburgh Airport (EDI)

Step 1: Tram or bus into Edinburgh Waverley Station.

Step 2: Direct train from Edinburgh Waverley to York (~2.5 hours).

Pro: The journey down through the coast and countryside is beautiful.

From Major UK Cities

From London

Direct train from King's Cross: 1h 50m (fastest), 2h 15m (average)

Operator: LNER (London North Eastern Railway)

Frequency: Every 30 minutes

Tip: Book "Advance Singles" online for cheaper deals than at the station.

From Manchester

TransPennine Express: Fast and frequent

Travel Time: 1h 25m to 1h 50m depending on service

Pro Tip: Sit on the right-hand side when heading to York for better countryside views.

From Leeds

A quick ride—only 20 to 30 minutes.

Trains run every 10–15 minutes.

Perfect if you plan to stay in Leeds and do a day trip to York.

From Edinburgh

LNER or CrossCountry trains provide direct services.

Journey time is just under 2.5 hours.

Arriving in York: Station Tips, Taxis, and Walking Routes

Once you arrive at York Station, you'll be greeted with clear signage—but here's what you won't see in the brochures.

York Station Orientation

There are two main exits:

Main (front): This takes you toward the city centre. Use this one.

Rear (via footbridge): Leads to long-stay car parks and a quieter road.

Author's Tip: Don't be tempted by shortcuts—just follow signs for the city centre or York Minster.

Taxi Tips

Taxi rank is directly outside the front of the station.

York taxis are metered and generally honest.

You don't need to tip drivers, but rounding up is appreciated.

Walking Distances from the Station

York Minster: 15 minutes

The Shambles: 12 minutes

Most city centre hotels: 10–18 minutes on foot

Museum Gardens: 8 minutes

Tip: Avoid dragging wheeled luggage over cobblestones. A backpack or rolling duffel is best for the old town terrain.

York Pass, Train Deals & Local Bus Hacks (2025 Updates)

The York Pass

What It Is: A digital or physical pass offering free entry to 25+ attractions (including York Minster, JORVIK Viking Centre, and Clifford's Tower).

Price: ~£55 for 1 day, £70 for 2 days, £85 for 3 days

Worth It?: Yes, if you plan to do at least 3 paid attractions per day.

Includes: Free hop-on-hop-off bus tour, discounts at restaurants and shops.

Tip: Don't activate the pass too early in the day—use it when you're ready to enter the first attraction, not when you board a train.

Train Deal Tips

Split Ticketing: Use websites like TrainSplit or SplitMyFare to save money by breaking your trip into multiple ticketed legs.

Railcards: If you're staying longer in the UK, buy a National Railcard (16–25, Senior, Two Together) for 1/3 off fares.

Advance Singles: Book at least 2–4 weeks ahead for major savings.

Pro Tip: Trains arriving before 9:30 AM on weekdays are "peak time"—avoid these unless you need to travel early.

Local Bus Hacks

First York Buses run the city network. Tickets start at £2 for a single journey.

Tap & Cap: Use contactless payment on buses—your daily fares will be capped automatically.

Park & Ride: If you're driving into York, park outside the city and ride the bus in for cheap and easy access.

Bus to Designer Outlet: York has a direct service to the McArthurGlen outlet mall—a 20-minute ride with good shopping deals.

Mistakes to Avoid When Arriving

Even experienced travelers fall into some common traps when arriving in York. Let's make sure you don't.

Mistake #1: Confusing Train Stations

York has one main station, but don't mix it up with Newark Northgate or Yorkshire towns like Selby or Harrogate when booking online. Double-check the station code: YRK.

Mistake #2: Taking the Wrong Station Exit

If you exit to the rear by accident, it adds 10–15 minutes to your walk. Always exit via the main concourse, and follow signs to City Centre / York Minster.

Mistake #3: Booking Tight Connections

Don't assume your train or flight will be perfectly on time. Avoid tight changeovers—especially at Leeds or Manchester.

Mistake #4: Buying Train Tickets at the Station

This is usually the most expensive option. Book online in advance (via Trainline, LNER, or National Rail) for much better prices.

Mistake #5: Not Preparing for the Walk

York's charm is in its streets, but those cobbles are unforgiving. Wear supportive shoes, pack light, and be ready to walk from the station to your accommodation.

Your Arrival, Done Right

Getting to York doesn't have to feel like a puzzle. With the right knowledge, you'll glide in with ease, confidence, and anticipation instead of stress. Whether you step off the train after a journey through golden countryside, or you emerge from a long-haul flight ready to be grounded in something real, York will be there—quiet, ancient, welcoming.

Now that you're here, let's begin. The real York awaits just a few steps from the platform.

Chapter 4

Where to Stay in York: Area Guide for All Budgets & Styles

Let me tell you something that no booking site will warn you about: where you stay in York can completely shape how you experience York.

This isn't London or Manchester where neighborhoods are miles apart and hopping on the Tube will save the day. York is intimate. You don't just "get around"—you walk it, you feel it, you stumble upon magic on the way to your morning coffee. That's why choosing the right place to stay isn't just about price or stars. It's about vibe, access, comfort, and whether you want to hear cathedral bells or riverside ducks when you wake up.

I've slept in centuries-old inns where floorboards creak with charm. I've stayed in sleek modern apartments where you can make a proper cuppa while watching the Minster glow at sunset. I've tried budget hostels and hidden B&Bs, and trust me—every one gave me a different York.

In this chapter, I'll walk you through York's key areas, personality by personality, so you can match your travel style with the right neighborhood. Then, we'll dive into specific hotel types, insider booking tips, and some honest pros and cons of hotels, B&Bs, and Airbnbs in 2025. Let's make sure your accommodation becomes part of your story—not a footnote.

Interactive Lodging Map: Match Your Style to the Right York Neighborhood

Think of York as a target with concentric circles. The closer you are to the center (inside the medieval walls), the more energy, history, and crowds you'll experience. The further out you go, the quieter, greener, and more "local" it feels.

Here's a guide to the main neighborhoods, each with its own traveler personality:

City Centre (Inside the Walls)

Personality: The History Buff, The First-Time Visitor, The Instagrammer

This is the beating heart of York—where you'll find The Shambles, York Minster, Clifford's Tower, and museums all within walking distance. Wake up to bells, sleep to quiet cobbled streets, and walk everywhere.

Pros:

Step outside and you're in 1,000-year-old history

Surrounded by cafés, pubs, and street performers

Zero transportation costs

Cons:

Can get noisy (especially near nightlife streets like Micklegate)

Prices are higher; parking is rare and expensive

Early check-ins are strict due to turnover demand

Bootham

Personality: The Romantic Couple, The Art Lover, The Solo Thinker

North of the Minster and outside Bootham Bar, this area feels like York's elegant escape. It's quiet, leafy, and full of Georgian townhouses.

37 | York Travel Guide 2025

Pros:

A 5–10 minute walk to the centre

Calmer, less touristy streets

Near Museum Gardens and the Art Gallery

Cons:

Fewer budget options

Some hotels feel formal or outdated without charm

Bishopthorpe Road ("Bishy Road")

Personality: The Hip Traveler, The Foodie, The Young Family

This is York's coolest neighborhood outside the walls. Locals love it. Independent cafés, markets, playgrounds, and brunch spots dominate the vibe.

Pros:

Less crowded, more local

Fantastic food scene and green spaces (Rowntree Park)

Affordable Airbnb options and guesthouses

Cons:

15–20 minute walk into town (though scenic along the river)

Some properties are small or attached homes with thin walls

Clifton

Personality: The Retreater, The Runner, The River Walker

Want peace? Head north to Clifton. Close enough for day-tripping into town, but far enough to feel residential and grounded.

Pros:

Near Clifton Ings for nature walks

Quiet, good for long stays

Homestead Park and York Observatory nearby

Cons:

Buses needed unless you like walking 30+ minutes

Fewer restaurants and shops

Micklegate & Blossom Street

Personality: The Night Owl, The Backpacker, The Second-Time Visitor

West of the station, this is York's gateway for rail travelers. The area is a mix of old pubs, budget inns, and young energy.

Pros:

Walking distance to the station and the centre

Cheaper hotels and great pub scene

Lively but not overwhelming

Cons:

Can be noisy at night

Parking is difficult

Heworth & Layerthorpe

Personality: The Long-Stayer, The Digital Nomad, The Peace-Seeker

East York is slower-paced, full of Victorian homes and quiet lanes. Ideal for travelers staying longer or working remotely.

Pros:

Larger accommodations

Local vibe, less touristy

Close to local groceries and quiet parks

Cons:

Longer walk (20–30 mins) to key attractions

Fewer dining options unless you head into town

Best Accommodation Types for Every Style & Budget

Best Boutique Hotels

The Dean Court Hotel – Overlooks York Minster. Historic but modern interiors.

Grays Court Hotel – 11th-century building, stunning gardens, and Michelin-rated restaurant

The Parisi Hotel – Creative, quirky, and independently run near the old walls

Most Romantic Inns & Stays

Middlethorpe Hall & Spa – A countryside manor just outside the city, perfect for couples

The Guy Fawkes Inn – Birthplace of Guy Fawkes, with candlelit rooms and medieval charm

The Churchill Hotel – Grand, stately, with vintage touches

Family-Friendly Accommodations

Staycity Aparthotels – Kitchenettes, space, and near the station

Novotel York Centre – Pool, river views, and kid-friendly dining

Airbnbs in Bishy Road or Heworth – Quiet and close to parks

Best Hostels & Budget Stays

Safestay York – Georgian townhouse hostel with dorms and private rooms

Astor York – Quirky, community-focused, with breakfast and big gardens

YHA York – On the riverside with modern facilities, great for solo travelers

Airbnb vs Hotel vs B&B: Pros, Cons & Hidden Costs

Airbnb

Pros:

More space, great for families or longer stays

Kitchens = food savings

Can feel more "local"

Cons:

Cleaning fees and service charges can surprise you

No reception = trickier check-ins

Some properties are illegally let—choose "Superhosts" with verified reviews

Hotel

Pros:

Easy booking, 24/7 service

Central locations

Often include breakfast

Cons:

Smaller rooms than Airbnbs

Prices jump during festivals and weekends

Can feel impersonal

B&B

Pros:

Authentic, friendly, hosted by locals

Home-cooked breakfasts

Often located in charming townhouses

Cons:

May have curfews or shared bathrooms

Limited availability during peak season

Not ideal for digital nomads needing workspace

Safety, Noise Zones & Walkability Tips

York is very safe, day and night. Violent crime is rare, and locals are friendly. But some areas are better suited for certain travelers than others.

Stay Safe By:

Avoiding isolated riverside paths late at night

Being cautious near Micklegate or Fossgate after midnight (pub noise)

Checking for working smoke detectors in old B&Bs or Airbnbs

Noise Zones to Note:

Shambles & Stonegate: Beautiful, but can be loud from 7 AM deliveries and 10 PM pub spillouts

Micklegate: Great pubs = great noise

Bootham & Clifton: Whisper-quiet at night

Walkability Insights:

Inside the walls = best for walking everywhere

Outside the walls = check if your hotel is on a hill or cobbled lane

Bishy Road & Micklegate are scenic walking routes into the city

Final Word: Make Your Stay Part of the Story

In York, your accommodation isn't just a place to sleep. It's a chapter in your experience. Do you want the echoes of a monk's footsteps in your hallway? The smell of croissants from the bakery below your window? The clink of a fireplace poker as the innkeeper brings you an extra blanket?

Whatever your travel style, there's a part of York waiting to welcome you home.

Choose it wisely—and it will elevate your trip from memorable to unforgettable.

Chapter 5

York's Essentials in 1–5 Days: Complete Daily Itineraries with Custom Maps

Let's face it—no one wants to leave York feeling like they missed something essential. Yet that's exactly what happens to most visitors. They spend too long in the wrong place, visit top sites at the busiest times, or don't build enough time into their day to just breathe in the magic of the city. York is not about ticking off a checklist. It's about feeling the rhythm of cobbled streets, listening to echoes in ancient churches, and letting history (and good coffee) guide your steps.

That's why this chapter exists: to hand you flexible, field-tested, real-world itineraries tailored to how long you're staying and what you're most excited to experience. Whether you're a one-day wanderer or a five-day deep diver, you'll find curated routes here designed to eliminate decision fatigue while maximizing joy.

Each itinerary includes:

Smart routing with walking times

Café and rest break suggestions

Best times to visit key attractions

Optional detours and secrets only locals know

Thematic versions for special interests: history, photography, kids, food, ghost stories

One Day in York: The Blitz Tour (Perfect for First-Timers & Day-Trippers)

Total walking time: ~2 hours (easy pace)

Focus: Must-see landmarks, local charm, and iconic photo ops

Best Day: Tuesday or Wednesday (fewer crowds)

08:30 AM – Start at York Train Station

Walk over Lendal Bridge as morning mist rises from the River Ouse.

09:00 AM – York Minster

Arrive early before the coach tours. Take your time—this is the largest Gothic cathedral in Northern Europe. Climb the Central Tower if you're feeling brave (and fit).

Best light for photos: morning sun on the west front.

10:30 AM – Treasurer's House (2 minutes walk)

A National Trust gem with Roman remains in the basement and perfectly preserved Edwardian interiors.

11:15 AM – Stroll through Dean's Park & Stonegate

Grab a snack from Bettys Tea Room's takeaway window.

Coffee break: Brew & Brownie – just across the river, worth the detour.

12:30 PM – Lunch in The Shambles Market Food Court

Try a Yorkshire pudding wrap or handmade pasta.

Midday is busiest—stand to the side for the best photos of the crooked buildings.

01:30 PM – JORVIK Viking Centre

A ride-through experience and archaeological goldmine. Kids love it. So do adults.

03:00 PM – Clifford's Tower

Climb to the top for panoramic views over York's rooftops.

04:00 PM – Museum Gardens & Yorkshire Museum

Stroll among Roman ruins, medieval walls, and flower beds.

You'll likely see squirrels and maybe a falconer training a bird of prey.

05:30 PM – Early dinner or drinks at The House of Trembling Madness (Lendal)

Local ales, wild boar pie, and a taxidermy-filled ceiling you won't forget.

07:00 PM – Ghost Tour

York is the most haunted city in Europe. The original Ghost Walk (since 1973) starts at 8 PM and is atmospheric, fun, and packed with history.

Three Days in York: The Explorer's Route

Ideal for those who want to explore history, food, and secret corners without rushing.

Day 1 – The Classics (same as the One-Day Itinerary)

Day 2 – Local Life & Hidden Gems

09:00 AM – Walk the City Walls from Micklegate Bar to Monk Bar

Panoramic views, hidden gardens, and medieval towers.

10:30 AM – Bar Convent Living Heritage Centre

A peaceful hidden museum and working convent with a charming café.

12:00 PM – Lunch on Bishopthorpe Road ("Bishy Road")

Local favorites: The Pig & Pastry or Robinsons.

__Optional picnic: Pick up supplies and head to Rowntree Park.__

02:00 PM – York Castle Museum

Time-travel through recreated Victorian streets, prison cells, and fashion exhibits.

04:00 PM – Explore Fossgate & Walmgate

This area is hip, artsy, and full of indie shops and bars.

06:00 PM – Dinner at Skosh

__A Michelin-guide modern British restaurant with small plates.__

Day 3 – History Meets Nature

09:00 AM – Yorkshire Museum (if missed earlier)

Roman, Viking, and medieval exhibits housed in Museum Gardens.

11:00 AM – Bootham Bar to St Mary's Abbey ruins

Optional detour to the York Observatory (small, but magical).

12:30 PM – Lunch at Café No.8 on Gillygate

Farm-to-table style in a tranquil garden.

02:00 PM – National Railway Museum

It's massive, free, and fascinating even if you're not into trains. Don't miss the royal carriages.

05:00 PM – Sunset walk by the River Ouse

Follow the riverside path from Lendal Bridge to Millennium Bridge and back.

Evening – Catch a show at York Theatre Royal or relax with live jazz at Sotano.

Five Days in York: The Deep Dive

You're the kind of traveler who wants to live York. Here's how to stretch your experience without a single dull moment.

Day 4 – Castles & Countryside

Day trip to Castle Howard – a Baroque masterpiece 30 minutes from York.

Lunch at the on-site café or in the charming village of Malton (a food lover's paradise).

Return by 5 PM and enjoy a quiet dinner at your B&B or hotel.

Day 5 – Thematic Day (Choose Your Adventure)

Thematic Itineraries (Tailored by Interest)

<u>For History Lovers</u>

York Minster

JORVIK Viking Centre

York Castle Museum

Bar Walls

Treasurer's House

Merchant Adventurers' Hall

Ghost Walk with historical focus

<u>For Instagrammers</u>

Shambles (early morning)

Clifford's Tower at sunset

St. Mary's Abbey ruins in golden hour

The city walls near Monk Bar

Stonegate with warm morning light

Hidden bookshops: Fossgate Books, The Portal Bookshop

<u>For Kids & Families</u>

JORVIK Viking Centre

York's Chocolate Story

Railway Museum (don't miss the train simulator)

Rowntree Park playground

Dig! (hands-on archaeology for kids)

For Foodies

Breakfast at Brew & Brownie

Lunch at Spark:York (street food market)

Afternoon tea at Bettys

Dinner at Roots (Michelin-starred, by Tommy Banks)

Craft beer tasting at Brew York

For Ghost Hunters

Ghost Merchant of York (buy your own handmade ghost!)

The Original Ghost Walk of York

Haunted inns: Golden Fleece, Guy Fawkes Inn

Snickelways like Mad Alice Lane and Coffee Yard at twilight

Don't-Miss Tips: Best Times for Photos & Fewer Crowds

York Minster: Go at 9 AM when it opens. You'll beat the tour groups.

Shambles: Arrive before 8:30 AM for that "empty medieval street" photo.

City Walls: Walk at sunset for magical golden light over the rooftops.

Museum Gardens: Best just after opening (10 AM), especially for photos of the Abbey ruins.

Clifford's Tower: Late afternoon for light, but early morning for fewer people.

River Walks: Go at twilight when the city lights reflect off the Ouse.

Final Word: Let York Reveal Itself at Your Pace

No matter how many days you spend here, the key is this: don't try to "conquer" York. Let it show itself to you. Let it slow you down. Let it surprise you with a crumbling arch you didn't expect, a second-hand book you fall in love with, or a ghost story you can't shake.

Whether you're blitzing through in 24 hours or savoring every cobbled step over five dreamy days, these itineraries are your compass—not your cage.

Now lace up your shoes, charge your camera, and turn the page.

Your York journey is just beginning.

Chapter 6

Immersive York: Top Attractions, Hidden Gems & Living History

I'll never forget the moment I first stepped inside York Minster. The hush that fell over me wasn't just about awe—it was about the deep-rooted realization that this city is not a museum; it's a living story still being written. York doesn't just preserve history—it invites you into it, lets you walk its layers, and rewards those who look beyond the obvious.

This chapter is your deep dive into York's most iconic experiences, yes—but also into its lesser-known wonders, quiet corners, local secrets, and ethical choices that let you enjoy this city respectfully. Whether you're the type who plans every stop or the wanderer who prefers to get lost and discover, York has treasures for both.

Major attractions (York Minster, Jorvik Viking Centre, The Shambles) explained without fluff

York Minster: A Cathedral Like No Other

Let's begin with the landmark that defines the skyline—and much of the city's soul.

York Minster is more than just a church; it's the spiritual and architectural heart of northern England. Built over a Roman fortress and completed over 250 years, this massive Gothic structure is stunning from every angle—but it's inside where the transformation begins.

Highlights:

The Great East Window—the largest expanse of medieval stained glass in the world.

The Chapter House, with its acoustic dome and intricately carved stone seats.

The Undercroft Museum, which walks you through 2,000 years of history—from Roman to Norman to medieval.

The Tower Climb (275 steps!)—for a panoramic view of the red-tiled roofs and Yorkshire hills beyond.

Best time to visit: 9:00 AM sharp when it opens. You'll beat the crowds and catch morning light on the stained glass.

Tip: Don't skip the audio guide or a live guided tour. Even locals discover something new every time.

JORVIK Viking Centre: Step into 10th-Century York

Built directly on the archaeological remains of Viking-era York (or Jórvík), the JORVIK Viking Centre is an immersive, sensory experience like no other.

Yes, there's a ride. And yes, it smells like fish and leather and woodsmoke—that's the point. You feel what life was like a thousand years ago, thanks to groundbreaking research and incredibly lifelike animatronics.

Don't Miss:

The glass floor displaying actual Viking-era streets

Live interpreters who can tell you what your name would've been in Old Norse

Artifact gallery with real items unearthed from Coppergate

Book tickets online in advance—queues are long year-round.

The Shambles: York's Most Photographed Street

Narrow, crooked, and impossibly charming, The Shambles is a preserved medieval street once used by butchers. The buildings lean toward each other like old gossiping friends, and small shop signs creak in the wind.

Today, it's filled with boutiques, wizarding shops (yes, there's a strong Harry Potter vibe), and local treats.

Local Tip: Step off the main drag into Shambles Market, a lively open-air market with street food, vintage finds, and excellent coffee at KREP.

Best photo spot: Stand at the corner near The Shop That Must Not Be Named, just after sunrise for empty streets and golden light.

Hidden Gems: York Beyond the Guidebooks

What makes York truly unforgettable isn't just the big names. It's the places tucked behind iron gates, hidden down narrow snickelways (York's version of alleyways), and whispered about by locals.

Barley Hall

A medieval townhouse restored to its 15th-century glory, complete with tapestries, carved beams, and interactive exhibits. Often missed, but incredibly atmospheric.

Theme: Living history

Located: Just off Stonegate

Why Go?: To sit at a medieval banquet table and learn what people really ate in 1480.

Roman Bath Museum

Beneath a pub—yes, a working pub—lies a real Roman bathhouse.

Theme: Roman archaeology

Located: Under the Roman Bath pub on St. Sampson's Square

Why Go?: Few tourists even know it's there. Order a pint, then descend into history.

Treasurer's House (National Trust)

A stunning historic home steps from York Minster, with a famously haunted cellar and one of the best tea gardens in the city.

Theme: Edwardian elegance and Roman foundations

Don't Miss: The Roman soldiers' ghost story, retold by staff who have actually experienced it.

Holy Trinity Church, Goodramgate

Slip through an iron gate near a pharmacy and you'll find yourself in a hidden garden and 12th-century church that feels like a sacred secret.

Theme: Serenity and soul

Why Go?: Worn box pews, candlelit corners, and silence—even during peak season.

Minster Gate Bookshop

A dreamy second-hand bookshop that feels like Diagon Alley inside. Books on everything from local folklore to Viking shipbuilding.

Lesser-Known Museums & Off-Grid History

York Castle Museum

Not so hidden, but often underestimated. Don't be fooled by the name—this is one of the most immersive museums in the UK. It includes:

Kirkgate, a recreated Victorian street

The original debtors' prison where highwayman Dick Turpin was held

Period rooms from Edwardian parlors to 1960s kitchens

DIG! (Archaeology for All Ages)

A hands-on museum where kids and adults can excavate fake trenches, touch real Roman artifacts, and feel like an archaeologist for the day.

Great for: Families, school groups, curious adults

Fairfax House

A beautifully restored Georgian townhouse with ornate plasterwork, paintings, and furniture that tell the story of 18th-century York's elite.

Ethical Travel: Supporting York with Respect

York's biggest challenge in 2025 is balancing tourism with preservation. Here's how to make your visit truly sustainable:

Do:

Buy from independent shops and avoid chain stores in historic areas

Stay at locally owned B&Bs or boutique hotels instead of large chains

Eat at local cafés and ask staff about their favorite spots—you'll get better food and better stories

Take walking tours with accredited Blue Badge guides

Donate to conservation efforts at the Minster, Barley Hall, or the York Archaeological Trust

Avoid:

Touching or climbing ancient walls or ruins—erosion is a real issue

Using drones in the city centre—it disturbs nesting birds and ruins the skyline for others

Feeding pigeons or ducks—it disrupts the ecosystem

Littering in snickelways or riverside paths, where cleanup is difficult

Final Thoughts: Make York Part of Your Story

You don't just visit York—you enter it. Its walls don't just encircle history—they invite you in. And if you listen closely—beyond the bells, the tour groups, and the market hum—you'll hear it speaking directly to you.

The trick to truly immersing yourself in York? Don't just see the Minster—sit with it. Don't just take a photo of The Shambles—get lost in its shadows. Don't just walk the walls—follow them as if they're leading you somewhere secret.

Because in York, they often are.

Chapter 7

Eat Like a Local: Pubs, Afternoon Teas, Bakeries & Beyond

If there's one thing I've learned about York after countless visits (and more Yorkshire puddings than I care to admit), it's that food here is never just food. It's memory, ritual, comfort, and culture—served on a warm plate with a strong brew or a cheeky pint. To eat in York is to taste centuries of tradition blended with today's foodie creativity.

Whether you're craving old-fashioned roast dinners by a fireside, warm baked goods from a medieval market lane, or vibrant plant-based plates served under string lights and indie music, York offers all of this—and it does so in a way that feels deeply authentic. In this chapter, we'll cover everything from iconic must-tries and historical pubs to halal bites, gluten-free goodies, and café etiquette that'll have you blending in like a local.

Iconic Foods to Try in York

Let's begin with the essentials. These are the dishes and treats that York locals grow up with—and visitors can't leave without tasting.

Fat Rascals

A local legend. Somewhere between a rock cake and a scone, Fat Rascals are fruity, buttery, and topped with glacé cherries and almonds. Think of them as Yorkshire's answer to afternoon tea's blandest offerings.

Where to try: Bettys Café & Tea Rooms (the original, and still the best).

Sunday Roast with Yorkshire Pudding

Yorkshire is the birthplace of this British institution. A traditional Sunday roast includes meat (beef is king here), roast potatoes, vegetables, gravy, and of course, the giant, fluffy Yorkshire pudding—essentially a golden-brown bowl made of batter to hold all that lovely gravy.

Where to try:

The Punch Bowl (Stonegate) – historic pub, hearty portions

Guy Fawkes Inn – intimate, candlelit, very local

The Refectory Kitchen & Terrace – more upscale and seasonal

Artisan Pies

Whether you're popping into a butcher's shop for a steak & stilton hand pie or sitting down to a slow-cooked lamb and rosemary pie in a gastropub, this city takes its pies seriously.

Where to try:

The York Roast Co. – famous for their Yorkshire pudding wraps

Piebald Inn (for a trip just outside York) – over 50 types of pies

Bennetts Butchers (Shambles Market) – takeaway classics

York's Chocolate Story

This is not just a tour—it's a historical culinary experience. York was once the chocolate capital of the UK, home to Rowntree's and Terry's. Learn the story and make your own chocolate.

Try this: Terry's Chocolate Orange-inspired desserts at local cafés

Best Places for Traditional Yorkshire Cuisine

York has held onto its roots. You'll find historic pubs that have served roast beef since the 1600s, cozy tearooms with lace curtains, and kitchens cooking with recipes passed down for generations.

Pubs & Gastropubs

The House of the Trembling Madness

Location: Stonegate & Lendal locations

Vibe: Medieval decor, taxidermy, craft beer

Try: Wild boar pie with mash and ale gravy

The Blue Bell

York's smallest and coziest pub

Serves real ale and simple but excellent pub snacks

The Black Swan

A 15th-century coaching inn

Try their steak & ale pie or fish & chips with minted peas

Afternoon Tea Spots

Bettys Tea Room

The ultimate Yorkshire afternoon tea. Vintage charm, piano music, tiered cake stands. Expect queues.

Try: Fat rascal, scones with clotted cream, and their signature blend tea

The Countess of York (at the Railway Museum)

Afternoon tea served in a restored Pullman train carriage

A memorable experience, especially for families or train lovers

The Ivy St Helen's Square

A modern take on the tradition, with plush interiors and seasonal menus

Vegan, Halal, Kosher, Gluten-Free & Budget Dining

York is an old city, but its food scene is refreshingly inclusive. Whether you have dietary needs, budget limits, or ethical preferences, there's something to suit you.

Vegan & Vegetarian

Humpit – A hummus and falafel bar inside the historic Shambles Market. Affordable, filling, and entirely plant-based.

Goji Café – Vegetarian café with vegan cakes, gluten-free dishes, and a warm atmosphere.

Source – Upscale vegan fine dining with seasonal ingredients.

Halal Options

While York doesn't have a huge selection, there are a few trusted halal-friendly spots:

The Yak & Yeti Gurkha Restaurant – Authentic Nepalese food with halal chicken and lamb options.

Shambles Kitchen – Ask about halal meats (they often rotate based on availability).

Phranakhon Thai Tapas – Not certified halal, but many non-pork dishes and vegetarian options are available.

Tip: York Mosque (Bull Lane) is a great place to ask about the most current and trusted halal eateries.

Kosher & Jewish-Friendly Options

York has a small Jewish community and limited kosher facilities, but several vegetarian cafés and bakeries can accommodate kosher-style diets. Always check with staff for ingredients and prep details.

Go-To Spots:

The Hairy Fig – Deli with locally sourced artisan goods, many vegetarian

The Pig & Pastry – Brunch spot with flexible menus (early arrival recommended)

Gluten-Free Dining

York is gluten-free friendly, with many spots offering alternatives that actually taste good.

Filmore & Union – Gluten-free baked goods, brunch dishes, and smoothies

Ambiente Tapas – Clear allergen labeling and GF-friendly options

El Piano – 100% gluten-free, vegan, and allergy-conscious (a rare gem)

Budget-Friendly Bites

Spark:York – Street food hub built from shipping containers. Vegan burgers, wood-fired pizza, bao buns—all affordable.

Shambles Food Court – Try Yuzu Street Food or Los Moros (North African cuisine)

Market Tavern Meal Deals – Traditional pub meals for under £10

Dining Etiquette, Tipping Norms & Menu Terms

Booking & Seating

Reservations: Essential for weekends, tea rooms, and fine dining.

Walk-ins: Accepted at pubs and casual spots, but you may need to wait.

Tipping Culture

Restaurants: 10–12.5% is standard for good service. Not always included in the bill—check the bottom.

Pubs & Counters: No tip expected unless full table service is provided.

Cafés: Round up or leave change if you liked the service.

Menu Terminology to Know

Mash = Mashed potatoes

Bangers = Sausages

Ploughman's = A cold lunch plate with cheese, pickles, and bread

Treacle = British syrup (sweet)

Black pudding = Savoury blood sausage (not a dessert!)

Pud = Pudding/dessert

Local Phrase to Know:

"Nowt fancy, but proper good."

Translation: It's not showy, but it tastes amazing.

Final Word: Eat with Curiosity, Leave with Crumbs on Your Chin

Eating in York is like stepping into the arms of a proud, food-loving grandmother—she wants to feed you, impress you, and maybe fatten you up a little. Every meal tells a story, whether it's being shared over candlelight in a timber-framed tavern or from a park bench with a pasty in hand.

So don't diet here. Don't rush here. And don't settle for the high street chains.

Ask questions. Try the odd-looking pastry. Say yes to the gravy. Share your table with a stranger at a crowded pub.

That's how York feeds you—not just with food, but with welcome, warmth, and a little extra butter on top.

Chapter 8

Shop, Stroll, Snap: Markets, Boutiques & Instagram Spots

There's something timeless about shopping in York. It's not about ticking things off a list or hitting the same shops you could find in any big city. Here, shopping is a slow stroll through storybook lanes, past crooked timber-framed buildings, window boxes overflowing with flowers, and the tempting scent of handmade fudge or fresh-baked bread.

In York, you shop with your eyes as much as your hands. You stop to read hand-painted signs. You duck into a narrow alley and emerge in a secret courtyard full of local makers. You pause—again and again—to take photos because every corner seems made for a camera.

This chapter is your personal map to the best places to browse, buy, and capture the soul of York. Whether you're after vintage treasures, rare books, handmade gifts, or just unforgettable views to fill your camera roll, I'll walk you through the spots that locals cherish and savvy travelers return to again and again.

The best local markets (Shambles Market, Bishopthorpe Road indie scene)

York's Best Local Markets

Let's start with the heartbeat of the city's shopping scene: markets. These are not tourist traps but living breathing community hubs—full of craftspeople, bakers, artists, and storytellers disguised as stallholders.

Shambles Market

Location: Just off The Shambles (between Parliament Street and Newgate)

Open: Daily, 7 am – 5 pm

This open-air market is a maze of over 70 stalls offering a mix of street food, local produce, artisan crafts, and handmade clothing. It's vibrant, authentic, and surprisingly affordable.

What to buy:

Yorkshire honey and chutneys

Hand-sewn leather journals

Ceramic mugs with York Minster motifs

Tiny ghost figurines from local artists (a York classic)

Foodie Alert: Grab a falafel wrap from Shambles Kitchen, a Korean chicken box from KREP, or a warm cinnamon bun from Bluebird Bakery.

Tip: Arrive mid-morning when stalls are fully open, but the lunch rush hasn't begun. Perfect for casual browsing and people-watching.

Bishopthorpe Road (aka "Bishy Road") Indie Scene

Location: South of the city centre, a short walk from the city walls

Best Days to Visit: Thursday–Saturday afternoons

Bishy Road is a haven for independent shops and community spirit. It's where locals go for a slow Saturday stroll, with coffee in one hand and a tote bag in the other.

Top spots:

Pextons – The kind of old-fashioned hardware store that sells everything from paintbrushes to plant pots.

The Pig & Pastry – Famous café and bakery with irresistible scones.

Frankie & Johnny's Cookshop – Quirky kitchenware and locally made treats.

Cycle Heaven – Even if you don't ride, the vibes (and coffee) are worth it.

This area is York's soul: creative, relaxed, and fiercely supportive of local business.

Vintage, Rare Books & Artisan Shopping

Skip the high-street chains and let's dive into the shops that define York's character.

The Minster Gate Bookshop

A multi-level maze of old wooden staircases, creaking floorboards, and shelves stuffed with secondhand and antique books. You'll find everything from 19th-century novels to forgotten travel guides from the 1950s.

Feels like: Discovering your grandfather's attic, if he were a literature professor.

York Ghost Merchants (on The Shambles)

Probably the most charming souvenir shop in the UK. They sell tiny, handcrafted ghost figurines, each unique and packaged with a mini certificate. Often there's a queue—but it's worth it.

Collectors tip: Check their Instagram before you visit to see what's in stock.

Dog & Bone Vintage

Location: Castlegate

An Aladdin's cave of vintage fashion, from leather jackets and 70s boots to sequined evening wear. Prices are fair, and staff genuinely care about helping you find the right look.

York Makers & Art Spaces

The Blue Tree Gallery – Beautiful contemporary local art

Pyramid Gallery – Handmade jewellery, prints, and ceramics

The Braithwaite Gallery – Framed illustrations and York-themed art

Snap-Worthy Spots: York's Most Instagrammable Corners

You don't need filters in York. The light, the architecture, and the unexpected charm of every side street do all the work for you. Here's a curated list of York's most photogenic locations—tried, tested, and crowd-approved.

York Minster – East Front

Why: Captures the full grandeur in morning light

Pro Tip: Stand near Dean's Park for a clear view with greenery framing the cathedral

The Shambles (at sunrise)

Why: The slanted buildings, warm tones, and shadows are dreamlike early in the day

Pro Tip: Position yourself just outside The Shop That Must Not Be Named for symmetry

Lendal Bridge & Museum Gardens

Why: View of the river, old stonework, and York's skyline all in one shot

Pro Tip: Cross to the opposite riverbank for a head-on photo of the Minster through the trees

York Railway Station

One of the most beautiful train stations in the UK, with long sweeping platforms, Victorian ironwork, and golden-hour magic.

Hidden Snickelways

Mad Alice Lane, Coffee Yard, and Lady Peckett's Yard are medieval alleys perfect for depth-of-field shots and moody edits.

Historic Doors & Secret Corners

Holy Trinity Church (Goodramgate): Ancient doorways and tranquil gardens

Barley Hall: Timber-beamed entryways with hanging lanterns

Tip: Use portrait mode on your phone for doors and windows, and wide-angle for alleys.

How to Shop Smart and Pack it Back Home

Whether you're flying home or taking the train, smart shopping means thinking ahead about weight, customs, and breakability. Here's how to do it like a pro:

Smart Buys:

Flat items: Art prints, postcards, handmade journals

Light textiles: Scarves, linen tea towels, or vintage ties

Food items: Sealed chutneys, fudge, or chocolate (Terry's or Rowntree's for a local touch)

Risky Buys:

Large pottery or ceramics (beautiful, but fragile)

Open liquids (like locally made oils or sauces)

Rare books over 100 years old (check customs rules)

Pro Packing Tips:

Wrap breakables in your clothing, not near suitcase edges

Use shoes to hold souvenirs like candle holders or ghosts

If you're flying carry-on only: Remember no liquids over 100ml and check duty-free allowances

Final Word: Strolling Is the Real Shopping

The magic of shopping in York isn't just in the bags you take home. It's in the conversations with a stallholder about how they make their soap by hand. It's in the slow pause outside a shop window that catches the golden light. It's in the way time seems to stretch on Bishy Road as you sip your coffee and watch the world pass by.

In York, shopping is not a task—it's a pleasure. And every market, every alley, every crooked storefront has something to give, if you take the time to let it surprise you.

So stroll, snap, and shop—but let the city guide you. Some of your best finds will come when you're looking for something else entirely.

Chapter

9

York Beyond the Centre: Day Trips, Countryside & Coastal Escapes

After a few days wandering York's cobbled lanes, soaking in Gothic grandeur and Viking lore, you may feel like you've seen the whole picture. But that's when the real adventure begins—when you step beyond the city walls. Because York is more than a destination—it's a gateway to some of England's most breathtaking countryside, storybook villages, and rugged coastal gems.

Whether you have just one extra day or are returning for a second visit and want to deepen your Yorkshire experience, this chapter will guide you through the very best day trips, multi-day excursions, and hidden escapes—without the stress of getting lost, caught in bad weather, or stuck with confusing train routes.

From the haunting ruins of Whitby Abbey to the rolling heather-covered moors of Brontë country, and from stately homes like Castle Howard to quiet seaside towns that feel frozen in time, this is your field-tested, story-rich, hassle-free guide to exploring York's glorious surroundings.

The Classics: Unmissable Day Trips from York

These destinations are all reachable within a day—many in just an hour or two—and they each offer a unique dimension of Yorkshire life and heritage. Let's start with three absolute standouts.

Whitby: Dracula, Abbeys & Dramatic Coastlines

Travel Time: ~2 hours by train (or 1.5 hours by car)

Best For: History lovers, literary buffs, seafood fans, and moody seascape photographers.

Whitby is where Bram Stoker's Dracula was born, quite literally. The dramatic ruins of Whitby Abbey loom over the town from a cliff, and the 199 steps leading up to it are as iconic as they are steep. But Whitby's charm goes far beyond gothic fiction.

Must-See:

Whitby Abbey – haunting and beautiful, especially at sunset

Captain Cook Memorial Museum – the famed explorer started his career here

The Harbour – fishing boats, sea birds, and cobbled charm

Fortune's Kippers – wood-smoked fish from a 19th-century smokehouse

Best Time to Go: April–September (avoid winter train delays and chilly sea winds)

Public Transport Tip:

There's no direct train from York—you'll need to transfer in Middlesbrough or take a scenic journey via the North Yorkshire Moors Railway (seasonal steam trains run from Pickering).

By Car: Take the A64/A169 route and allow time for winding coastal roads.

Castle Howard: England's Finest Stately Home

Travel Time: ~40 minutes by car or 1 hour by bus

Best For: Garden lovers, architecture buffs, and fans of Bridgerton or Brideshead Revisited

Set amidst rolling parkland, Castle Howard is a masterpiece of baroque architecture, fountains, and opulent interiors. The estate is vast—expect to spend a full half-day here exploring.

Don't Miss:

The Great Hall and Atlas Fountain

Walled rose garden and woodlands

Farm shop and café (great for lunch)

Public Transport Tip: Bus #181 runs from York during peak season (check updated timetables on Castle Howard's site).

Driving Note: There's free parking, and roads are well-marked. Book tickets online to skip queues.

North York Moors: Wild Walks & Heather Dreams

Travel Time: 1–1.5 hours by car

Best For: Hikers, nature lovers, literary souls (think Brontë and James Herriot)

The North York Moors National Park is a sea of wind-whipped heather, ancient dry-stone walls, ruined abbeys, and friendly market towns. It's the kind of landscape that invites poetry—or at least a thermos and walking boots.

Top Spots:

Goathland – aka "Hogsmeade Station" from Harry Potter

Rosedale Abbey – tiny village, big views

Helmsley – market town with castle ruins, ideal for lunch

Farndale – famous for springtime daffodils

Car Essential: This region is best explored with a vehicle. Be mindful of single-track roads and sheep crossings.

What to Pack: Waterproofs, layers, walking shoes, offline maps—signal can be patchy.

How to Travel Without the Stress

Whether you're using public transport or hiring a car, getting beyond York doesn't have to be a logistical nightmare—if you plan wisely.

Public Transport Tips

Trainline App – Reliable for tickets, live delays, and platform changes

Coastliner Bus – One of the UK's most scenic bus routes, running from Leeds through York to Scarborough and Whitby

Advance Tickets – Book train tickets early for major savings

Off-Peak Travel – Fewer crowds, cheaper fares (after 9:30 am on weekdays)

Car Rental Without Headaches

Renting a car in York can give you access to rural gems public transport can't reach—but it comes with fine print.

☐ **Do:**

Rent from York Railway Station (easy pickup/drop-off)

Choose an automatic if you're not used to driving on the left

Use Google Maps offline or Waze with real-time updates

☐ **Avoid:**

Parking in central York (tight spaces, high fees)

Unmarked rural roads after dark

Forgetting to refuel before returning the vehicle (check your fuel policy)

Local Tip: Many villages have no petrol stations—plan fuel stops before heading into the moors or dales.

Cultural Etiquette Outside the City

Rural Yorkshire is warm and welcoming—but it moves at a gentler pace. Here's how to travel respectfully:

Greet people when entering shops or pubs—"Hiya" or "Morning" goes a long way

Close gates behind you when hiking or entering farms (respect the "Right to Roam" rules)

Be patient—locals may chat longer in shops or cafes; it's part of the charm

Don't block lanes with parked cars or stop in the middle of roads for photos

Ask before photographing people or private homes, even if they look quaint

Yorkshire hospitality is genuine—but so is their pride in keeping things tidy, quiet, and neighborly.

Sample Itineraries: 1–2 Day Countryside Escapes

Planning to stay longer? Here are two suggested countryside getaways to soak in Yorkshire's rural richness.

Itinerary A: 1-Day North Moors Loop (by Car)

08:00 AM – Depart York

09:15 AM – Coffee in Helmsley, visit Helmsley Castle

11:00 AM – Drive to Rievaulx Abbey (monastic ruins in the woods)

01:00 PM – Picnic lunch in Farndale or pub in Hutton-le-Hole

03:00 PM – Stop in Goathland (Potter fans rejoice)

05:00 PM – Return to York before sunset

Best in spring/summer for scenery and wildflowers

Itinerary B: 2-Day Coastal Getaway

Day 1: York to Whitby

Arrive by noon

Explore Whitby Abbey, harbour, and 199 Steps

Enjoy fish & chips at Magpie Café

Stay overnight at a seaside B&B or quirky guesthouse

Day 2: Whitby to Robin Hood's Bay & Back

Morning hike along the Cleveland Way (coastal cliffs)

Stop at Robin Hood's Bay, a tiny smuggler's village

Return to York via scenic A171 road

Ideal for romantic breaks or solo soul-recharging

Final Thoughts: Open the Map, Follow the Wind

Stepping beyond York is like turning the page of a centuries-old novel—suddenly, you're not just visiting, you're living the landscape. You're sipping tea in a market town pub that's stood since the Tudors. You're walking in the footprints of monks, authors, and pirates. You're breathing in air that rolls fresh off the moors, tinged with the scent of bracken and sea salt.

These escapes don't replace York—they complete it.

So bring your boots, keep your camera close, and let the road (or rail) take you beyond the centre—where Yorkshire opens wide and waits with wild beauty, stories, and a welcome just as warm as its historic heart.

Chapter 10

Stay Confident: Practical Tips, Local Etiquette & Travel Smart

Traveling to a historic city like York should feel like stepping into a beautifully preserved storybook, not stumbling through a logistical minefield. From navigating public transport to understanding social cues and staying connected, this chapter is your confidence compass. Whether you're a first-timer looking to feel safe and informed, or an experienced traveler aiming to blend in with locals, this guide equips you with everything you need to travel smart, respectfully, and with ease.

York may be ancient, but the way it supports modern travelers is refreshingly up-to-date—when you know how to tap into it. From Wi-Fi to walking etiquette, LGBTQ+ travel to healthcare access, here's how to make your trip smooth, secure, and satisfying in 2025.

Staying Connected: Internet Access, SIM Cards & Power Plugs

In today's world, a phone with internet access is more than a luxury—it's a lifeline. Good news: York is a very digitally friendly city.

Internet Access

Free Public Wi-Fi: York offers free city Wi-Fi called CityConnect in the city centre, including popular areas like The Shambles, Parliament Street, and around York Minster.

Cafés & Pubs: Most independent cafés, such as Spring Espresso or The Perky Peacock, offer fast, password-protected Wi-Fi. Just ask at the counter.

SIM Cards & Data

Best UK SIM Options:

EE – best coverage

Vodafone – reliable and tourist-friendly packages

Three – great for international data roaming

Where to Buy: York Railway Station's WHSmith or mobile stores on Coney Street

Tip: If you're visiting from outside the UK, an unlocked phone is essential to use a UK SIM.

Power Plugs

Plug Type: Type G (three rectangular prongs)

Voltage: 230V / 50Hz

Travel Tip: Bring a universal adapter with surge protection. British plugs are large and may not fit all multi-port devices.

Travel Safety, Medical Help & Insurance in the UK

York is one of the safest cities in the UK for tourists, but confidence comes from being prepared. Here's how to handle the "just in case" scenarios.

Safety Tips

Crime Risk: Low. Petty theft is rare, but watch your bags in crowded spots like The Shambles Market or train stations.

Police: Dial 999 in an emergency or 101 for non-urgent help. Police presence is friendly and visible.

Medical Services

Emergency Care: York Hospital is a full-service NHS hospital, just 15 minutes' walk from the city centre.

Pharmacies: Boots (Coney Street & Monks Cross) is best for prescriptions and travel health essentials.

Minor Ailments: Visit a walk-in clinic or a chemist (pharmacy); they often have in-store consultation rooms.

☐ **Travel Insurance Advice:**

EU travelers: Bring your GHIC (Global Health Insurance Card) for emergency NHS treatment.

Non-EU travelers: Buy comprehensive travel insurance covering health, theft, and delays.

Local Etiquette: How to Respect York's Historical and Religious Spaces

York is proud of its deep cultural and spiritual history. From ancient churches to quiet memorials, it's important to know how to engage respectfully.

Churches & Cathedrals

York Minster: Entry is ticketed unless attending a service. Keep voices low, remove hats, and don't photograph during prayer or choir times.

Smaller churches (e.g., Holy Trinity Goodramgate): Free entry, but donations are welcome. Avoid phone use and dress modestly.

Historical Sites

Do Not Touch: Stone walls, artifacts, and museum displays are not to be leaned on or touched.

Photography: Always ask if flash is permitted. In some museums, photos are banned in entire exhibits.

Language: Politeness is key. "Please," "Thank you," and "Excuse me" go a long way with Yorkshire locals.

Local Behaviour Tip: In York, queuing is sacred. Never skip a line, even at a bus stop or food stall.

LGBTQ+ Travel Tips: Welcoming, Safe, and Celebratory

York is widely considered LGBTQ+ friendly, with a strong local queer community, annual Pride celebrations, and inclusive venues.

LGBTQ+-Inclusive Spots

The Portal Bookshop – A queer-owned store known for LGBTQ+ titles and inclusive events.

The Fossgate Social – Chill, inclusive café-bar often frequented by the creative community.

The York LGBT Forum – Offers resources and community support.

York Pride is held every June and features a vibrant parade through the city, with family-friendly events, concerts, and local participation.

Safety Tip: Public affection is generally safe in York, especially within the city walls. Still, stay aware in late-night pub areas like Micklegate after hours.

Solo Travel & Accessibility: Confidence for All Travelers

York is not only safe—it's also friendly for solo travelers and increasingly aware of accessibility needs.

Solo Travel

Locals are helpful and open, especially in independent shops, galleries, and cafés.

Walking alone at night is generally safe within the city centre—just stick to well-lit areas like Gillygate and Stonegate.

Guided tours (ghost walks, food tours, walking groups) are a great way to meet fellow travelers.

Accessibility

York Minster: Fully accessible with lifts and accessible toilets.

City Walls: Only partly accessible due to steep steps and narrow walkways.

Public Transport: First Bus York vehicles are wheelchair-accessible; most drivers will offer extra time and help.

Hotel Booking Tip: Always request ground-floor rooms or lifts in advance—many historic buildings don't have elevators.

Avoiding Tourist Traps & Common Scams in 2025

York is not plagued with scams like major global cities, but like anywhere, it's important to shop smart and dodge overpriced or low-quality experiences.

Tourist Traps to Skip

Overpriced chain restaurants near the Minster—choose independent spots like Roots or El Piano instead.

Generic souvenir shops on The Shambles—go for artisan markets and local makers instead.

Unlicensed street performers asking for large donations—appreciate but don't feel obligated to tip.

Travel-Smart Moves

Buy attraction tickets online in advance (like JORVIK or the York Dungeon) to avoid inflated same-day prices.

York Pass: A great value for multiple attractions, but only if you plan to use at least 3–4 in a day.

Google Reviews & Local Forums: Use them to double-check restaurants, pubs, or ghost tours before booking.

Insider Trick: Visit shops off Petergate and Fossgate for better quality, lower prices, and more genuine encounters with locals.

Final Word: Your Passport to Peace of Mind

Staying confident while traveling in York is about more than remembering your charger or knowing the right tipping etiquette. It's about understanding the spirit of a place—how people live, how history breathes, and how the city invites you to share in its rhythm without rushing or guessing.

In 2025, York offers something rare: the ability to travel with your heart wide open, knowing you're in a place where people want you to feel welcome. This chapter gives you the tools. But it's your mindset, your preparation, and your respect for the city's rhythm that will turn your trip from pleasant to profound.

So walk tall, stay curious, ask questions, and always leave room in your day—and your heart—for the unexpected.

York will take care of the rest.

GOODBYE TO YORK

95 | York Travel Guide 2025

Chapter 11

Conclusion: Your York Adventure Starts Now

As you reach the final pages of this guide, I want to speak to you not just as an author, but as a fellow traveler—someone who knows the feeling of anticipation before a journey, the excitement of exploring somewhere new, and the bittersweet pause when it's time to say goodbye. York is one of those rare places that doesn't just fill your itinerary—it fills your heart.

Whether you're standing before the vast stained-glass beauty of York Minster, wandering beneath medieval archways on a quiet morning, or sipping tea in a crooked, centuries-old café, there's something unforgettable about the way York moves at its own pace and rhythm—and invites you to join in.

Let's wrap up with a final note of guidance and inspiration—so you leave York not only with memories and mementos but also with no regrets and a full sense of satisfaction that your journey mattered.

Final Travel Wisdom for First-Timers

If you've never been to York before, here are some parting thoughts that will ensure your experience is truly rewarding—beyond the checklist, beyond the Instagram shots, beyond the guidebooks.

Let York Come to You

First-timers often make the mistake of rushing from attraction to attraction, trying to conquer every top 10 list. But York is a city best discovered through its slower moments—those chance encounters with a local shopkeeper, that unexpected story from a tour guide, or the quiet beauty of a morning fog rolling over the city walls.

Slow down. Look up. Wander on purpose. Let York tell you its story.

Be Ready to Step Off the Path

The most magical moments in York often happen off the beaten track. Maybe it's a quiet alley with a wrought iron sign that leads to a hidden courtyard. Or a secondhand bookshop that pulls you into an hour-long conversation about Viking history with the owner. Plan your days—but leave room for detours.

Ask Questions, Start Conversations

York is a city filled with proud locals—many of whom have roots that go back generations. Whether you're in a pub, a bookstore, or a museum, you'll find people who love to share their knowledge. Ask how something was made. Ask what the weather was like in 1962. Ask where they buy their cheese. It's the people who will bring the city to life.

Encouragement to Slow Down & Savor York's Stories

Too often, travelers arrive in York expecting to "do" the city in a day or two. But this is not a city meant for haste. York has stood for over two thousand years—what's the rush?

Spend 20 minutes just watching people in King's Square. Listen to the street musicians echo off the walls of Stonegate. Sit on a bench in the Museum Gardens, between Roman ruins and Victorian greenhouses, and imagine the lives that came before yours on this very spot.

York rewards the traveler who takes their time. Not with fireworks or fanfare, but with a deeper richness: the gentle unfolding of stories, layer after layer.

When you sit in the quiet of Holy Trinity Church, with its slanted pews and flickering candles, or walk a quiet stretch of the Bar Walls at dusk, you'll feel it—not just history, but a sense of being exactly where you are meant to be.

How to Leave York With No Regrets

You can't do everything. And you shouldn't try to.

But you can leave York knowing you've done it right—with these simple principles:

✔ Prioritize Experience Over Efficiency

It's better to fully enjoy five things than to rush through fifteen. Allow yourself to savor a moment, whether it's a quiet breakfast or a conversation with a ghost tour guide.

✔ Keep a York Journal

Even if it's just a few lines a day. What you noticed. What surprised you. What made you smile. York is a memory-maker—you'll want to capture the small moments before they fade.

✔ Don't Be Afraid to Come Back

York isn't a one-time city. Many travelers (myself included) return again and again, each time uncovering new layers, new legends, new loves. If you didn't get to do everything, consider it an invitation—not a failure.

"Travel isn't always about crossing off destinations—it's about returning to the ones that feel like home."

Resources for Further Reading, Travel Tools & Local Tours

If your York adventure is just beginning—or if you're planning your return already—these resources will help you dig deeper and travel smarter.

Recommended Reading

"York: A Rare Insight" by Ian D. Johnson – A rich look into the people behind the city's historical sites.

"Dracula" by Bram Stoker – Reread the classic after visiting Whitby Abbey for a fun literary connection.

"The Time Traveller's Guide to Medieval England" by Ian Mortimer – Offers incredible context for the streets you'll walk.

Useful Apps

Google Maps (Offline Mode) – Essential for the winding streets and hidden lanes.

Trainline – For real-time train info and ticket booking.

GetYourGuide – For last-minute tours and day trips around York and beyond.

YorkMix – A local news and events site with insights into festivals, food markets, and more.

Local Tours Worth Booking

The Bloody Tour of York – The city's most beloved ghost tour with theatrical storytelling.

York's Hidden History Walking Tour – Small group tour into the city's lesser-known landmarks.

JORVIK Viking Centre Guided Experience – Offers context and access beyond the standard exhibit.

Emergency Contacts & Local Help

Tourist Information Centre: 1 Museum Street (across from York Minster)

York Hospital: Wigginton Road – open 24/7

Non-Emergency Police: Dial 101 (for assistance, lost property, etc.)

Emergency Number: Dial 999 (for police, fire, or ambulance)

The Journey Begins Here

At the start of this guide, I told you that York is more than a city—it's a story. Now that you've reached the end, I hope you see that this story isn't over.

In fact, it's just beginning.

Maybe it starts with a sunrise walk along the Ouse. Or your first bite of a warm fat rascal. Maybe it's a quiet moment standing under the stained glass of the Great East Window, heart full and silent.

Wherever your York journey takes you, walk it with curiosity, humility, and an open heart.

The ghosts of York may whisper in the stone, but the stories they tell are yours to carry forward.

Now pack your bags, charge your phone, print your boarding pass—or maybe just close your eyes and picture the old city walls once more.

Your York adventure starts now.

Go write your chapter.

Chapter 12

Frequently Asked Questions (FAQs) – York Travel Guide 2025

*e*very traveler has questions before arriving in a new destination—and York, with its deep history, cobbled lanes, and cultural layers, often raises more than a few. Whether you're traveling solo, coming with family, staying for a weekend, or using York as a base to explore the rest of Yorkshire, this section gathers the most frequently asked questions and provides clear, reliable, and experience-backed answers.

These FAQs are based on real visitor inquiries, local insight, and up-to-date 2025 travel advice to help you plan with confidence and avoid any unnecessary surprises.

GENERAL TRAVEL QUESTIONS

Is York worth visiting in 2025?

Absolutely. In fact, 2025 is one of the best times to visit York. The city has seen several enhancements in recent years—new walking tours, digital visitor passes, improved accessibility, and modernized museum experiences—while still preserving its medieval charm. York has also strengthened its sustainability and inclusivity efforts, making it an even more welcoming destination for global travelers.

How many days do I need in York?

For a first-timer:

1 Day: A compact blitz of key highlights (York Minster, The Shambles, a city wall walk, and a museum)

2–3 Days: Ideal for a deeper dive with a walking tour, multiple museums, and relaxed meals

4–5 Days: Perfect for combining city exploration with day trips to places like Castle Howard, Whitby, or the Yorkshire Moors

Is York good for solo travelers?

Yes, it's an excellent solo travel destination. York is compact, walkable, and very safe. There's also a rich offering of guided walking tours, independent cafés, and day trip opportunities, making it easy to meet locals or fellow travelers without ever feeling isolated.

ARRIVAL & TRANSPORTATION

What is the easiest way to get to York from London or Manchester?

From London: Take the LNER or Grand Central train from London King's Cross. It takes just under 2 hours.

From Manchester: Take the TransPennine Express directly from Manchester Piccadilly (~1.5 hours).

Both stations drop you off at York Station, a short walk to the city centre.

Do I need a car in York?

No, you don't need a car to explore York city centre. In fact, driving in the historic core is discouraged due to limited parking and narrow streets. However, if you plan day trips into the countryside, renting a car may be worthwhile.

Is the York Pass worth buying?

Yes—if you plan to visit multiple attractions in one or two days, the York Pass offers excellent value. It includes access to York Minster, JORVIK Viking Centre, Barley Hall, city tours, and more. Always compare the cost of individual entries to your planned itinerary to ensure value.

ACCOMMODATION & AREAS TO STAY

What's the best area to stay in York?

City Centre: Ideal for first-timers and sightseers; close to major attractions

Bootham/Clifton: Quieter, elegant neighborhoods close to York Minster

Bishopthorpe Road ("Bishy Road"): Trendy, local vibe with great food and indie shops

Fishergate: Budget-friendly and family options outside the walls but walkable

Are Airbnb and B&Bs reliable in York?

Yes. York has a strong tradition of well-run B&Bs, and Airbnb options range from cozy apartments in medieval buildings to luxury lofts. Be sure to check for hidden cleaning or service fees, and always verify reviews before booking.

FOOD, DRINK & DINING ETIQUETTE

What food is York known for?

Fat Rascals – Giant fruity scones from Bettys Café

Yorkshire Pudding – A classic side with roast dinners

Parkin – Ginger-spiced cake popular in autumn

Fish & Chips – Best enjoyed riverside or near the Shambles

Do I need to tip in York restaurants or cafés?

Tipping is appreciated but not mandatory. If service was good, a 10–12.5% tip is the norm. Some restaurants include a service charge—always check the bill.

Can I find vegan, halal, kosher, or gluten-free options in York?

Yes, York's culinary scene has become very inclusive. Top spots include:

Vegan: El Piano, Goji Café

Halal: The Rice Shack, Turtle Bay

Kosher-friendly: Ask ahead; Jewish community centers are limited but options exist

Gluten-Free: Source, Filmore & Union (clearly labeled menus)

MONEY, INTERNET & PRACTICAL TIPS

What currency is used in York?

British Pound Sterling (£). Credit and debit cards are widely accepted, including contactless and mobile payments. Small shops or markets may still prefer cash for purchases under £5.

Is there free Wi-Fi in York?

Yes. The CityConnect network offers free Wi-Fi across the city centre, including near York Minster, Parliament Street, and The Shambles. Most hotels, cafés, and attractions also offer free Wi-Fi.

What type of plug does the UK use?

The UK uses Type G plugs (three rectangular pins). Voltage: 230V. Bring an adapter if you're coming from the US, EU, or most of Asia.

Are public toilets available? Are they clean?

Yes, York has several well-maintained public toilets in the city centre (some require a small fee, like 40p). Many cafés and museums also have clean facilities.

SAFETY, HEALTH, INSURANCE & EMERGENCIES

Is York safe for tourists?

Extremely. York is one of the safest cities in the UK. Petty crime is very low. Still, take standard precautions with your belongings, especially in crowded areas.

Do I need travel insurance for York?

Yes—always advisable. Non-UK visitors should have travel insurance that covers health emergencies, lost luggage, and trip cancellations. EU visitors should bring their GHIC card for NHS access.

What should I do in a medical emergency?

Call 999 for immediate assistance (police, ambulance, fire).

York Hospital is open 24/7. For non-urgent health needs, visit a pharmacy or walk-in clinic.

INCLUSION, LGBTQ+ & ACCESSIBILITY

Is York LGBTQ+ friendly?

Yes. York is an inclusive and welcoming city with LGBTQ+ cafés, bookshops, and an annual Pride festival. Public displays of affection are generally safe.

Is York accessible for wheelchairs or those with limited mobility?

Yes—with some exceptions. York Minster, museums, and many modern venues are fully accessible. However, cobbled streets and narrow historic buildings can be challenging. Use access-friendly maps and contact hotels/tours in advance for accommodations.

Final FAQ Wisdom: Still Unsure? Just Ask

York is a city full of helpful people, from shopkeepers to tour guides to hotel staff. If you're ever confused, lost, or uncertain, don't hesitate to ask—most locals are more than happy to help, and they take pride in their city's hospitality.

Whether you're holding a map in the rain or looking for the best fish pie on a Tuesday night, someone in York will likely smile, give you directions, and even walk you there.

That's the spirit of York—rooted in kindness, history, and curiosity.

And now that you've got the answers, it's time to go and make your own.

HAPPY TRAVEL, SAFE TRIP!

Printed in Dunstable, United Kingdom